STARTING WORK
for Interns, New Hires, and Summer Associates

MARY CRANE

100 Things You Need To Know™
Starting Work
for
Interns,
New Hires,
and Summer Associates

by Mary R. Crane

Cover design: Merryall Studio
Interior design: Diana Russell Design
Author photo: Tony Gale
Editorial consultant: Holly Brady

ISBN-13: 978-0-9890664-0-2

The series title *100 Things You Need To Know*
and its logo are trademarks of Mary Crane & Associates.

Address permission requests to:
Mary Crane & Associates
New York, NY
info@marycrane.com

For more information about
Mary Crane & Associates:
www.marycrane.com

Contents

Introduction

Earlier this year, l was asked to create a presentation for a group of young adults about to begin their first internships. After consulting several employers, all of whom regularly invite interns into their offices, I created a list of 75 things every intern should know before heading off to work. Later, one of my law firm clients reported that she found the list applicable to the summer associates who had just completed a two-month stint in their office. And one of my corporate clients insisted that his new hires could benefit from this knowledge, too.

Weeks after creating my initial list, I debriefed the interns. I asked them: What didn't I tell you? And if you had known that one thing, how would your internship have been easier or more productive?

Thus, this listing of 100 things you need to know before you start work reflects the combined knowledge of employers, summer associates and interns, as well as my own thoughts.

As you read this book, please keep the following in mind:

■ Some of the concepts that follow may seem extremely simplistic. You already know you should say "please" and "thank you" (see #23). Yet, when confronted with pressing deadlines and difficult assignments, many interns, summer associates and new hires forget to say these words, and trust me, they can make or break important business relationships.

- I suspect your parents, teachers and career advisors have discussed other principles with you. For instance, the odds are pretty good that lots of people have told you to be cautious when posting online (see #58). Yet, no matter how many times experts say, "Don't post anything online that you would feel uncomfortable seeing on the front page of *The New York Times*," people who should know better (professionals, famous golfers, even a U.S. Congressman) email and text inappropriate material.

- Some suggestions are more complex than others. This book reviews basic table manners (see #42). However, in order for you to make the most of any business lunch or dinner, you have much more to learn. Look for future books in this series to learn how to manage business meals, make the most of networking events, manage your time and get along with others at work.

Congratulations, you're about to enter the world of work!

This is an important first step in the transition you will undertake from being a student to becoming a successful professional. You have a plethora of challenges ahead of you. Over the next several weeks, you will begin to learn the intricacies of a new profession. You will start to develop a professional persona. Your position as a summer associate or intern will allow you to lay the foundation of what will eventually become your professional network. Perform well and your introduction to the world of work may lead to a coveted job offer.

So roll up your sleeves and get ready to work.

Following are "100 Things You Need To Know" to be a successful intern, summer associate or new hire.

Chapter 1

Before Your Job Begins

You wouldn't begin a vacation without first doing some preliminary planning. (At least I hope you wouldn't!) Where will you go? To the beach? To the mountains? Will you drive or fly? Where will you stay? Can you afford a fancy resort, or is a budget hotel a better choice? How will you fill your few precious days of downtime?

It's equally important that you undertake some preliminary planning before you enter the world of work. Remember, you will never accomplish a goal that you don't set. Before your first day at work, establish specific goals. Research the organization and your supervisor. Gather together everything you will take to work and check your Day-One outfit. Then, grab a good night of sleep and get ready to go!

1. Establish S.M.A.R.T. goals

A S.M.A.R.T. goal is one that is Specific, Measurable, Achievable, Realistic and Time-targeted.

A summer associate assigned to a law firm's mergers and acquisitions practice group might set the following S.M.A.R.T. goal: by the end of the summer, research, draft bylaws and articles of incorporation, and participate in creating plans for at least one merger.

In contrast, an investment bank intern might set the following S.M.A.R.T. goal: once a week, review a randomly selected financial statement and build a leveraged buyout model from scratch.

Or a new hire on Capitol Hill might set this S.M.A.R.T. goal: by the end of the year, develop effective working relationships with all members of the Senator's personal staff, meet all staff members of the legislative committee to which the Senator has been assigned, and help draft one bill.

While an intern in the fashion industry might set this S.M.A.R.T. goal: in a two-month period, identify the most important players within the design studio and understand their roles, identify leading industry competitors, and create a calendar of key fashion industry events.

Identify what you hope to accomplish in the limited time of your internship or during your first year at work. Once you have been assigned specific tasks, be prepared to review and revise these goals.

2. Research

Learn everything you can about the law firm, company, government entity or organization. Understand the products or services it provides. Is it a large, international firm or a small, family-owned entity? Through its web presence, can you discern anything about its culture? Does it appear to be a workplace where employees are expected to wear suits? Fashion-forward clothing? Or is it a jeans-and-T-shirt employer? Does it actively promote any hands-on contributions it makes to the local community? Is it environmentally friendly?

Create a work journal, in paper or electronic format, and add your research results. Throughout your internship, time as a summer associate, or first year of employment, add to this journal, developing an ongoing record of the people you meet and projects assigned to you. Make note of new contacts, skills acquired and lessons learned.

3. Make contact with your new employer

Reach out to the person who runs your intern, summer associate or new hire program. Determine whether you will be the organization's only new employee or one of many.

Use this conversation or email exchange to confirm expectations regarding attire. Don't be surprised to learn that the clothing you have worn to school may not be appropriate at work. (Even if you've landed a position with an Internet start-up, don't even think about wearing torn jeans to work.)

If you need additional clothing to dress appropriately for work, go shopping now!

See Chapter 8 for information regarding appropriate attire for work. For now, be assured that you don't need to spend a fortune to dress correctly. Confirm that you own enough tops (blouses or shirts) and bottoms (slacks and/or skirts) to wear a fresh outfit to work each day. These outfits must be clean, with no stains, no holes, no missing buttons, and all hems affixed. If you will work in an office setting, you should also own a tailored jacket or blazer and a couple of stylish sweaters.

4. Meet others

Have you learned that you will be one of several interns, summer associates or new hires? Has your employer forwarded a list of the others who have accepted a similar position, and their contact information? If so, reach out to the other people with whom you are about to begin work. If you happen to be located in the same city or town, consider meeting before your first day of work. If you do, on Day One you will already know at least one other person.

View this as an important first step to building your professional network. Throughout your career it's absolutely critical that you establish contacts and create sponsors, well-positioned people who will actively promote you and help you achieve your goals. So, get in the habit now. Do everything you can to start making connections before you even begin work.

5. Research your supervisor

If you know the name of your direct supervisor, search the organization's website for his or her bio. Then, go beyond the entity's website and continue your research. Google or Bing your supervisor's name. Can you pinpoint any of his or her other interests? Is she on the board of directors of the city art museum? Is he listed as a volunteer with a local soup kitchen? Look for your supervisor on LinkedIn.

When you undertake this research, for heaven's sake, be discrete. Learn everything you can about the people with whom you'll work, but don't get pegged as a cyber-stalker.

Understand, too, that your immediate employer, as well as all future employers, will search for information about you on various social networking sites. In fact, employers increasingly view this kind of research as their legal responsibility. Calling up your Facebook page and verifying your online persona is one of the ways they can mitigate potential legal liability.

Take time to clean up your Facebook page today. Go to each social networking site on which you or a friend has posted information about you, and confirm that the content is work-appropriate. Anything that an employer finds online should position you as a professional ready to enter the world of work. If it does not, pull it down now.

6. Respond to inquiries from your employer

Before you start work, your organization's Human Relations (HR) department may reach out to you with questions. For example, some organizations email their new hires and ask whether anyone has specific diet restrictions or food allergies. These factors are then taken into account when ordering meals served during orientation.

Promptly reply to these inquiries. In a world in which employers complain about a lack of professionalism among their newest workers, responding in a timely manner distinguishes you as a true professional.

Be aware that the people responsible for hiring new graduates increasingly do complain about a perceived lack of professionalism among applicants. The York College of Pennsylvania Center for Professional Excellence 2013 Professionalism Study, an online survey of HR professionals, noted the following:

- 44.6% of respondents believe the work ethic has gotten worse among new hires.
- 86.6% complain of new professionals adopting a "too casual" attitude towards work.
- 71.5% say new hires are not self-driven.
- 69.3% believe today's new hires lack ownership of their work.

7. Do a commute test run

It's absolutely critical that you arrive at work on time every day, and especially on your first day of work. A week before you start work, do a test run. Whether you plan to walk, ride a bike, drive, or take public transportation, test the length of your commute from where you live to your employer. It's better to arrive a little early and walk around the block than to be late.

I cannot overemphasize the importance of this one recommendation. On Day One, your employer will develop his or her first impression of you and your work habits. Employees who arrive late create an impression that work is not a priority—it's something they'll get around to when it's convenient. In contrast, the employee who undertakes a test run demonstrates an ability to anticipate and plan for potential problems. Anticipating problems is a skill, and it's one that can quickly distinguish you. Besides, your test run will help ensure that you arrive at work on Day One feeling calm and confident.

Make this commitment: *I will never be late for work!*

8. Check your Day-One outfit

The day before you start work, select the outfit you intend to wear to work. In Chapter 8, we'll address appropriate dress for work. For now:

- confirm that the outfit you have selected is clean, pressed, and does not require mending;

- if you've purchased a new jacket or blazer, remove any threads used to tack the rear vents closed;

- check that your shoes are polished and the heels are not worn;

- determine whether you need a haircut or a tidying-up of your current hairstyle.

9. Pre-pack a work kit

Your work kit should contain a comb or brush, breath mints, a pad of paper and a pen, and an energy bar (to get you through late morning hunger pangs or an afternoon energy slump). Make sure your wallet contains a picture ID and your Social Security card. If you require any medications, pack enough to get you through your first week.

When you arrive at work, you will probably be asked to provide "emergency contact information." (If you trip and break an ankle, should your employer contact Mom? Dad? A roommate?) Carry those names and their contact information with you, also.

Finally, pack something (a special photo on your smartphone, a good luck token) that will help you smile and relax when your nerves feel on edge.

If you work in an office setting, carry all of the above in a professional tote or computer bag. Remember, you are making the transition from school to work. Leave behind the backpack you've carried around campus, and use a tote that communicates you're a professional.

10. Get energized

Go to bed early and grab a good night of rest. I'm serious about this. You don't want to sleep through your first day at work!

If you're paranoid, set two alarm clocks. (Whenever I have an early-morning flight, I set both an alarm clock and the alarm on my smartphone!)

Then, get ready for the fun to begin!

Chapter 2

Welcome to Day One

The big day has arrived! You're about to start work.

Make a great first impression by arriving precisely on time and appropriately dressed. Attend any orientation that your employer offers. Meet your new boss. Put your head down and begin to work.

11. Create a positive first impression

You never get a second chance to make a first impression, and once made, it's nearly impossible to change. What's more, most people develop their first impressions in a split second.

On Day One, make the best first impression possible. Arrive precisely on time, put a big smile on your face, summon up all the confidence you have, and walk through the front door.

Throughout the entirety of your professional career—and especially now, at the beginning, make every effort to avoid creating the following impressions:

- I am entitled.
- I am better than anyone else.
- I am not a team player.
- I have a fragile ego.
- I know more than my employer.
- I deserve praise and recognition for completing my assignments.

12. Attend orientation

You may be asked to attend a Day-One orientation program. Pay close attention to the orientation facilitator. He or she will explain key policies and procedures, including: when your workday begins and ends; designated lunch hours; confidentiality expectations; and the appropriate use of company equipment, technology, and supplies.

If you will be compensated, you will likely be told how (by check or by direct deposit) and when you can expect to receive your first payment.

Make sure you leave orientation with a clear understanding of the rules and regulations for requesting hardware and software. You may be free to request a smartphone or laptop on your own, or a supervisor may need to do this on your behalf.

13. Introduce yourself professionally

Be prepared to introduce yourself to your new supervisor and other staff members. Each time you introduce yourself, state your name and your position.

Hi, I'm Ali Fahed. I've just joined the firm's environmental practice group.

or

Good morning. I'm Michael Suarez, the firm's newest financial analyst.

At the same time that you make these statements, make eye contact and extend your right hand. Now, you're ready for a handshake. Gently grasp the other person's hand, pump once or twice, and then release.

Sounds easy, right? What can be easier than shaking hands? Yet, I bet at least once in your life you and everyone you know has received a limp-wrist, cold-fish handshake. To avoid these, when you extend your right hand, hold it perfectly perpendicular to the ground. Once your hand falls over to a 45-degree angle, it's much easier for someone to grasp your little fingertips—something you definitely don't want.

14. Meet your fellow employees

If you are one of several new employees, and if you did not meet your fellow interns, summer associates or new hires before Day One, make every effort to do so during the orientation. Develop good working relationships with fellow employees as quickly as possible.

Remember: you may be the smartest person in the room, but if you don't work well with others, few organizations need you.

Don't expect everyone to warm up to you immediately. Studies estimate that somewhere between 16% and 50% of us are introverts, people who reenergize in solitude rather than by socializing with other people. Invest time in developing trust and building relationships with everyone at work. And don't forget, your manager may be an introvert. Be prepared to adjust to his or her quieter approach to work.

If you happen to be an introvert, commit to spending some part of your day socializing with others. Respect your need for peace and quiet, but recognize that you must comfortably interact with others in order to complete important work projects.

15. Remember names

As you are introduced to other employees, do everything you can to remember their names. This may be among the biggest challenges you will encounter during your first week at work.

Try using one of the following techniques:

Play any word relationship game that works for you. I happen to have three brothers, one named Bill, another named Tom, and one more named Joe. If I happen to meet someone named Bill, Tom, or Joe, in my mind's eye, I see my brother standing next to the person until I am able to say to myself, *I see my brother Bill—and that person's name is Bill.*

Use mnemonics. Someone's name may allow you to create a unique mental image. Use that image to help you remember the name. So, for example, when you meet me and learn my last name is Crane, picture me standing next to a whooping crane. Or alternatively, picture me standing next to a construction crane. The image may help you remember my last name.

Use repetition. Repeat the other person's name, at least three times in normal conversation. Please do *not* meet someone and immediately say, "Brandon, Brandon, Brandon, Brandon, Brandon, Brandon . . . I got it, your name is Brandon." Rather, as part of a normal conversation, repeat Brandon's name a number of times.

Here's how a conversation might go:

Hi, I'm Brandon Wheeler. I'm responsible for making sure all your technology needs are met.

Hi, Brandon. I'm Sarina Carter, the new product management intern, and I'm so glad to meet you. I understand I need to be accessible via a smartphone 24/7.

Got it. Let's see if we can get you a BlackBerry by close of business today.

I'd really appreciate that, Brandon. By the way, I've never used a BlackBerry before. Could you show me how to use one?

That shouldn't be a problem. I'll stop by your workstation later this afternoon.

Thanks, Brandon, I can't tell you how much I appreciate your help.

That's it. Sarina has repeated Brandon's name three times, and the conversation hasn't sounded awkward at all.

16. Ask others about their "stories"

Eons ago, I worked with someone who was especially adept at remembering other people's names. Eventually I summoned up some courage and asked him how he did it. His reply: "I used to be horrible at remembering names. But now, whenever I meet someone, I just ask them to 'tell me something about you.'" As long as he had a story to latch onto, he improved the odds of remembering the name to which it was connected.

Use this technique to create your own memorable introductions. What stories can you tell that position you as a person who is motivated, able to overcome challenges, and persistent?

A summer associate once told me about working on the legislative staff of a member of Congress. She had butted heads with the staff director, and she recognized these confrontations could negatively affect her career. She decided she needed to find some common ground.

After discovering that her supervisor was a closet *Gilligan's Island* fan, she invested a weekend watching reruns of the 1960s sitcom. Soon thereafter, at a weekly staff meeting, the summer associate referenced a *Gilligan's Island* episode. Immediately, she began to build rapport with the legislative director. From then on, she said, they got along famously.

What's the significance of this anecdote? Five years after hearing her story, I still remember that summer associate. Create your own stories.

17. Be prepared

From Day One forward, whenever you are at work, always carry a pad of paper and a pen.

Caveat: please do not carry your pen and paper into the office bathroom.

Every time you walk down a hallway, enter someone's office, or attend a meeting, you may be asked to perform some task:

Please deliver these proofs to Julia in the marketing department, get an update on the status of the website relaunch, and confirm that all employee bios have been reformatted.

I need you to attend the employee interviews at our IP litigation client. The interviews will start this Thursday and should run through next week. Check with Holly regarding the location. Also, see if the paralegals have pulled together backgrounders on each employee.

I need you to do the following three things quickly: book a flight so that you can accompany me to a client meeting leaving early Tuesday and returning late Thursday—check with my admin, who knows whether I'm flying Delta or United; book a hotel for Tuesday and Wednesday evening; and grab everything you can find on the domestic/global brand strategy we've created for these guys. I want us to review it before we take off.

By carrying pen and paper, you can immediately record requests and assignments as they are made. This will help eliminate your need to ask a supervisor to wait or to repeat a request. Furthermore, it lessens the likelihood that you will make a mistake due to a faulty memory.

18. Enjoy a Day-One lunch

On Day One, your supervisor or someone else in the organization may offer to take you to lunch. Or you may be served lunch as part of the orientation program. We'll address table manners in Chapter 5. For now, if you are asked to lunch, gather your personal gear and go, taking your best manners with you.

When you arrive at the restaurant, keep the following in mind:

■ As you review the menu, avoid the most and least expensive items.

■ Disregard any menu offering that will be messy to eat or that you don't know how to eat.

■ No matter what your hunger level is, be prepared to order the same number of courses that your supervisor or host orders.

■ With regards to beverage options, stick with iced tea, water, soda or fruit juice.

■ If you and your supervisor have both headed to lunch wearing jackets or suit coats, as long as your supervisor continues to wear his or her jacket, you should do the same.

■ If your supervisor has extended the invitation to lunch, you can assume that he or she will pay for your meal.

19. Show interest and enthusiasm

Always demonstrate a willingness to learn, and show enthusiasm for any work that is assigned to you. This includes the most menial tasks. If someone asks you to spend an entire first week reviewing documents in a windowless room, treat the assignment as if it's the most important project ever known to mankind.

Keep this in mind: you will never know where a menial task may take you.

Eons ago, when I attended the Culinary Institute of America, all students were required to complete an eight-month externship. For an aspiring chef, the position was the equivalent of an internship in a corporation or a summer associate position in a law firm. I secured a position at The Greenbrier, a lovely, old resort in White Sulphur Springs, West Virginia. I was among the lowest ranking people in the kitchen, and as such, I was assigned every miserable, unglamorous task you can imagine.

One year later, I was offered the opportunity to work in the White House kitchen. To this date, I am absolutely convinced I received that job offer mostly because of an attitude that consistently communicated, *I'll gladly tackle any task you assign to me.*

20. Avoid watching the clock

You may speed through Day One, rushing from an orientation to your first meeting with your supervisor, where you receive your first assignment, which you take to your brand new desk and immediately wonder, *How in the world am I supposed to do this?* It's equally possible that your first day will drag on at an interminably slow pace. After all, your supervisor doesn't know your capabilities yet, and he or she may hesitate to give you anything but the simplest assignments. Don't worry. As you demonstrate your abilities, more challenging work likely will come your way.

As your first workday nears its end, avoid being the first person out the door. Wait until you see others pack up their personal effects. Then, before departing, stop by your supervisor's office or workstation, update him or her on the progress you made on assigned tasks, and ask if it would be appropriate for you to close down for the day.

Chapter 3

Working With Others

With the exception of certain group projects, your success as a student has been largely based on your individual effort. Now that you've entered the world of work, oftentimes you will be evaluated by how well you work with others.

Psychologists spend their entire lives trying to understand people's behaviors. Without extensive training, you need to understand what motivates your supervisor and coworkers, and any hot-button issues that might set them off. If you succeed, you'll become immeasurably more valuable to your employer. If you fail, you'll be pegged as someone who "doesn't play well with others."

21. Be a team player

So much of your success at school is measured by how well you perform on individual projects. You either score well on a test or you don't. In the world of work, you will frequently be assigned to group projects, where your success will be dependent on how well the group performs. Always demonstrate a willingness to roll up your sleeves and pitch in.

When working with a group on a particular project, unless your direct supervisor pulls you from the project, stick with it until the project is completed.

Support other members of the team. When someone suggests a method for tackling a task, hear him or her out. When others ask for your help, jump at the opportunity. If a supervisor pulls someone from your project, be prepared to double your efforts.

When you disagree with a team member, manage your divergent views professionally. Openly address them. Do not ask your supervisor to mediate disagreements, and don't play political games. Demonstrate your ability to create win-win solutions.

22. Treat everyone respectfully and professionally

In most U.S. work environments, employees address each other by their first names. However, when working with someone who is much more senior than you (think your grandparents' ages), use the social titles of "Mr." or "Ms."

If you have been employed by a global concern, be prepared to address employees in other countries using their formal social titles. For example, German men frequently greet each other with "Herr (last name)," even when they've worked together for years.

Once anyone asks you to address him or her by a first name, by all means, do.

Avoid interrupting other workers when they speak.

Do not distract others from their work by talking loudly in the hallways or on your smartphone.

Think about your coworkers even when packing or picking up a snack or meal to be eaten in the office. Avoid smelly foods (anything with lots of garlic or onions, some cheeses, fish, even some vegetables—such as cabbage or asparagus) and foods that make noise when eaten (potato or corn chips).

23. Be courteous

Say "please" when you ask for something and "thank you" when something is given to you. When members of your workplace go out of their way to help you—even if it's someone on the nighttime cleaning crew—thank them.

If you want to make a big impression, handwrite a thank-you note. It's easy. Here's all you need to write:

Dear _____,

*Thank you very much for...*describe what they did.
Describe how it was important to you.
Tell them how you would like to follow up.

Sincerely,
Your name

At the end of the summer, a summer associate might write to a practice group leader:

Dear Nigel,

Thank you for giving me the opportunity to help with the Smirnov trial preparation in Russia. I am astounded with how much I learned about Russian criminal procedure in such a short time. I very much hope I will have the opportunity to work with you again upon my graduation from law school.

Sincerely,
Mary

An intern in the finance industry might write the following thank-you note to her supervisor:

Dear Alison,

Thank you for inviting me to cocktails in your home. I enjoyed spending some free time with my fellow analysts, and I especially enjoyed meeting the head of the firm. I hope we have additional opportunities to get together throughout the summer.

Sincerely,
Arnav

24. Assume everyone knows more than you do

Listen and learn from everyone, and I do mean every single person you encounter. You will be amazed what a night watchperson, a coffee stand worker, or a mailroom clerk can teach you about the inner workings of an organization.

As to administrative and support staff, they probably know more about the work you need to accomplish than you do at this stage in your career. These coworkers can make or break you. Give them lots of reasons to want to see you succeed.

25. Be prepared to flex to different work styles

Some of the people with whom you will work will have a bottom-line orientation. They'll want you to provide answers without extensive explanations. When following up with them, get to the point quickly and use short sentences.

Others will want you to brainstorm. When following up with these people, be prepared to suggest alternative strategies.

Still others will want you to provide them with lots of data and detail. When following up with these supervisors, bring an answer and all of the supporting data that you have collected.

Understanding the work styles of the people who surround you and adjusting to their wants and needs may be one of the greatest challenges you will encounter throughout your career. It takes a lifetime for some people to learn that there is no one right way to work with other people. Successful workers constantly adjust their own behaviors to work within the style preferences of their supervisors and fellow employees.

26. Ask lots of questions

When you are assigned a task, make sure you understand what has been requested. Don't be afraid to repeat it back:

Okay, let me make sure I understand. You want me to . . . .

At the same time, look for opportunities to demonstrate your ability to solve problems on your own. If you experience difficulties altering a PowerPoint presentation, do not automatically interrupt your supervisor's workday. Instead, try to find a solution. Google or Bing the issue that has arisen. Ask another intern or summer associate. Text the company's tech helpdesk. Check with an office manager. Demonstrate your ability to produce results.

27. Attend meetings

When you are asked to attend meetings, review any agenda beforehand. Arrive on time. If you are asked to contribute, be prepared to do so. Stay on point and add value. Ask informed questions.

Take notes. Record any action items given to you. Confirm and clarify the expectations of other meeting attendees.

Know expectations regarding smartphone use during a meeting. Some organizations frown on junior members glancing at their smartphones during the course of a meeting. In these cultures, meeting attendees are expected to be fully present, so it's a good idea to turn off your smartphone. In other organizations where employees are expected to be accessible 24/7, meeting attendees generally participate in discussions with their smartphones turned on.

Understand the culture that you have joined and adhere to its rules.

28. Never repeat gossip

Inevitably, you will hear some workplace gossip. Do not repeat one word of it. Don't repeat it in person, and definitely, don't repeat it in email or via a social networking site, such as Facebook or Twitter. Remember, any email you send can become a public document. Should you decide to share gossip via email, it may be forwarded to your supervisor and everyone else in your office. It may also be printed and become a permanent part of your employee file.

Before you say or type anything about your employer or a fellow employee, keep in mind the confidentiality agreements that you've signed.

Closely adhere to any company policies regarding social media, picture taking, etc.

29. Speak professionally

Ensure everything you say in the workplace is fit for public consumption. If you wouldn't say it to your grandmother, don't say it at work. Never use obscenities in the workplace. Don't make vulgar comments or jokes. Do not say or do anything that shows a lack of tolerance.

Learn how to speak succinctly. Stay on point, expressing the information you need to convey or request as simply as possible.

When you're unsure what to say, pause. A sentence interrupted by a second of silence sounds more professional than a meandering statement tied together by meaningless space fillers, such as "like," "um," and "you know."

At the end of each sentence, do not allow your voice to inflect upwards, which makes you sound uncertain of what you just said.

Please eliminate "no problem" from your conversations at work. Whenever an employer asks you to perform a task and you reply, "No problem," you have effectively devalued the work. Instead, say, "Right away" or "I'd be happy to."

30. Avoid offending others

If you offend someone, apologize immediately. Let the person know it was not your intent to be hurtful.

If another employee says or does something that offends you, respond with style. Consider saying: "I respectfully disagree," or "I wish you had not acted in that manner, but let's move on."

Chapter 4

Managing Your Time and Projects

Successful new professionals turn in quality work in a timely manner. Start each day with a game plan. Know what you will accomplish and when. Avoid interruptions during your most productive hours. Above all, manage others' expectations. When unforeseen delays develop, immediately inform your supervisor.

Be prepared to make mistakes. I like to remind myself that, if I don't make a mistake now and then, I'm no longer learning. When you do make a mistake, quickly own up to it.

31. Create a daily game plan

Begin each day at work with a written or recorded plan of the projects you need to complete. Prioritize those projects. Which must be completed first? Estimate how much time each project will require.

Everyone has an internal clock that dictates when he or she is most alert and capable of tackling tough mental projects. Most of us peak around 10:00 a.m. If you're one of these people, schedule tasks that require lots of brainpower between 9:00 a.m. and noon.

It's possible that you're the exception to this rule. You may be a late starter. Know when you are most alert, and tackle your toughest projects during that time. However, understand that ultimately you must complete projects in a timeframe that satisfies your employer's needs and expectations.

Record your daily game plan in your journal. In fact, add everything related to work—assignments, contacts, to-do lists—to your journal (see #5). Keeping critical information in one place improves efficiency. Avoid wasting time searching through piles of paper or walls of post-it notes.

If you choose to keep an electronic journal, perform backups religiously. Don't allow a crash to obliterate all of the data you've collected.

32. View every assignment as an opportunity

Each assignment gives you the opportunity to demonstrate your knowledge and talents. Initially, you may be asked to tackle mundane tasks. Remember that once you demonstrate an ability to perform a simple task well, you increase the likelihood that you will be assigned more challenging work.

Treat even the simplest assignment as if it's the most important one you've ever received.

Show initiative. Once you complete an assignment, don't hesitate to ask, "What's next?" or "How else may I help?"

33. Manage competing assignments

U se every assignment to demonstrate your talents and your willingness to work.

Once everyone in the office knows that you're a proven performer, other senior people within the organization may seek to assign tasks to you. If you end up reporting to multiple people, and they are unaware of your workload, work with everyone to prioritize your projects.

Understand that once you accept an assignment, it's yours. No one else is responsible for its completion. Should one assignment keep you from completing another assignment that you have accepted, you are the person at fault.

Always act like the consummate professional. When faced with two conflicting assignments, gather key players together, explain the situation, and work to negotiate a solution that satisfies everyone.

34. Tackle roadblocks

Have you hit a roadblock? Inevitably you will. A senior lawyer may ask you to find the most recent Canadian rules regarding climate change. You successfully locate the rules and discover they're written in French, a language with which neither you nor the senior lawyer is fluent. Or a supervisor may ask you to locate a buyer segmentation analysis. When you phone the relevant analyst, you discover he's taken a one-month sabbatical.

Every time you hit a roadblock, be prepared to plow through.

A successful summer associate would immediately take the French version of the Canadian rules to the firm's library and seek assistance in locating an English translation.

Similarly, the intern in search of a particular buyer segmentation analysis should contact the organization's information management team and request a copy of the report.

35. Understand your supervisor's priorities

While working on projects, it's better to ask questions than to make a potentially costly mistake.

Suppose a supervisor asks you to fly to a meeting in another city. What's most important? Does she want you to obtain the least expensive ticket—one that may require multiple stops—or does she prefer you to book a flight that's fast and direct, though more costly? Unless you understand these priorities, you risk making an important error.

On a day-to-day basis, your supervisor's priorities may vary. With each assignment, understand the following:

- overall goal of the project;
- measures of success;
- specific deadlines;
- available resources;
- acceptable costs;
- others involved in the specific assignment, and in any larger work product.

36. Email vs. face-to-face contact

Sometimes a quick face-to-face conversation will help you resolve outstanding issues faster than a series of email exchanges. When you find yourself sending a third email about a particular task, consider picking up the phone or walking down the hallway for a quick conversation.

Beyond speeding up the resolution of outstanding issues, there are plenty of other reasons for you to seek out opportunities to have face-to-face conversations at work. In Chapter 6, we'll address the importance of using your new job to begin building your professional network. At the core of every professional network are a series of one-on-one conversations that have contributed to the creation of a professional relationship.

In a high-tech world moving at hyper speed, never underestimate the impact of a simple conversation.

37. Take pride in your work

Every assignment you submit reflects upon you. Even when a supervisor has requested a "draft," use correct spelling, grammar, and punctuation. Never rely upon spell-check.

Before you turn in an assignment, print it out and undertake an additional review. You are more likely to see errors on hard copies than electronic files. Check and recheck all calculations. An investment bank supervisor reviewing comps that jump from $3 million to $300 million to $30 million in the span of three years may question the accuracy of an intern's work.

Before you turn in a printed document, make it neat. Never turn in an assignment that's stained by your morning coffee or afternoon lunch.

38. Meet all deadlines

View deadlines as sacrosanct. Once you accept an assignment with a designated deadline, only a genuine emergency (for example, a hurricane that knocks out the city's electrical grid) excuses your failure to meet it. As for emergencies, genuine professionals invest time imagining what could possibly go wrong and creating appropriate response plans.

In some cases, your ability to meet a deadline may be affected by other team members who have been assigned to the same project. Simply reminding another team member that you need his or her input to complete a project does not free you from the ultimate responsibility of completing that project on time.

When you encounter unexpected delays, inform your supervisor as soon as possible. Carefully manage others' expectations.

39. Own up to mistakes . . . immediately

Everyone makes mistakes. You will make them. Your supervisor will make them. Every employee in your organization, every customer and client, every person in the world makes mistakes.

With regard to mistakes, two factors distinguish professionals. First, they acknowledge their errors. They never slip into denial or fail to accept responsibility. Second, they learn from their mistakes and do not repeat errors unnecessarily.

When you make a mistake, own up to it immediately. Approach your supervisor *in person* and explain the situation. Do not use email. Owning up to a mistake shows that you hold yourself accountable, builds trust and enhances your credibility. Furthermore, fessing up quickly increases your supervisor's ability to take remedial action.

Never attempt to cover up a mistake. Most employers will excuse an honest mistake. They rarely forget a botched cover-up.

And never, ever blame someone else for your mistake.

40. Schedule regular feedback

To the extent your supervisor has time, ask to meet with him or her at the end of each week to receive feedback on your performance. Openly receive any feedback provided, especially criticism. No supervisor will provide constructive feedback unless he or she is interested in seeing you grow and develop. Listen carefully. Ask questions to confirm your understanding. Determine how you can improve your performance.

A quick reality check: although every organization I know encourages its managers to provide feedback, not everyone excels at this. Eventually, you will encounter a supervisor who will tell you, "Assume everything is okay. If there's a problem, I'll let you know."

When this occurs, explain your need to learn and grow. If that doesn't elicit more detailed feedback from your supervisor, reach out to your peers and anyone else with whom you interact at work to acquire a better understanding of how you can improve your work performance.

Chapter 5

Managing Social Events

In addition to working hard, you may be invited to a variety of social activities, such as business meals or office parties. Make sure you attend these business-related social events. They are intended to be relaxing and fun, and they are an important way for employers to connect with you.

However, never forget that these are business events, requiring you to act in a business-appropriate manner.

41. Respond quickly to social invitations

You may be asked to attend a variety of social events, ranging from a simple lunch at a local diner to a fancy cocktail party at the CEO's penthouse apartment. By all means, attend. These are important opportunities for you to connect on a social basis with a variety of people in the company or organization.

As soon as you are invited to an event, check your calendar and confirm your availability. Do not wait for a better offer! This holds true whether the invitation is via a quick email ("Want to grab a bite of lunch today?") or a more formal printed invitation.

If an R.S.V.P. is requested ("Please R.S.V.P. by calling Mike Barnes in HR, ext. 2435"), call and indicate whether or not you will attend.

Once you have indicated that you will attend, only an absolute emergency excuses your absence.

42. Know table manners

Before you attend a business lunch or dinner, brush up on your table manners. Let's cover a few here:

■ Do not place your sunglasses, smartphone or anything else on a restaurant tabletop. Ladies, if possible, hold your handbag in your lap. If it's too large, place it as near to your feet as possible.

■ As soon as you sit down, unfold your napkin and place it in your lap. Throughout the meal, before you drink any beverage, take your napkin and gently tap your lips. Your goal is to wipe away anything (crumbs, sauces) that could be transferred from your mouth to glassware. During the course of a meal, if you need to excuse yourself, place the napkin on your chair. At the end of the meal, place your napkin on the tabletop.

■ If you find lots of silverware at your place setting, work from the outside in. Once you use a piece of silverware, do not place it back on the table. Instead, rest it on your plate.

■ Your bread and butter plate is located on the upper left side of your place setting. When you eat bread or a roll, break off a portion equivalent to one or two bites, butter that portion, and then eat. Do not break a roll in half and slather butter over the entire half. Use your bread and butter knife only to spread butter. Never use it to cut a roll.

■ If the waitstaff places any food item near you, offer it first to the person with whom you are dining. So, for example, with a basket of rolls or a plate of lemon slices, offer the item to others before taking your own.

43. Follow your host's lead

When you've been invited to a meal and you're unsure what to do, mimic your host or hostess.

Should you order both an appetizer and a main course? Order the same number of courses that your host or hostess orders.

If the waitstaff requests your order before they approach your host or hostess, ask for both an appetizer and an entrée. Should your host or hostess order an entrée only, you can always ask the waitstaff to revise your order and skip the appetizer.

Avoid creating the situation in which your host dines, while you sit with nothing to do, or *vice versa.*

Avoid ordering the most or least expensive item on any menu.

At a business lunch, skip alcohol altogether. When the waitstaff requests your beverage order, ask for iced tea, soda or water. At a business dinner, you may enjoy a glass of wine or a beer, depending on the style of the restaurant.

At this stage in your career it's probably best to skip cocktails and other drinks made with high-octane liquor at business functions. And don't feel pressured to drink. If you don't consume alcohol, for whatever reason, that's perfectly fine.

44. Avoid creating the appearance of someone who has lots of special needs

If you are allergic to certain foods or ingredients, by all means, make the waitstaff aware. However, at business meals, keep quirky food preferences to yourself. No one wants you to go into anaphylactic shock from eating peanuts. But at the same time, they don't need to know about your aversion to green foods.

If, after you've tasted the food you ordered, you find you're not crazy about your selection, eat what you can. However, if the waitstaff delivers something that you did not order, inform them. Another diner may be waiting for that meal.

When a course is delivered to the table, wait for everyone to be served before you begin eating.

Throughout the course of the meal, keep pace with other diners. If you find that you always finish first, slow down. Periodically, put down your fork and engage in conversation instead of eating. In contrast, if you find that you are consistently the last diner to finish a course, learn to pace yourself accordingly. As soon as you see that a majority of the dining party has completed a course, you're done, too!

45. Avoid tricky and risky foods

Avoid ordering any "tricky" food that you're not sure how to eat. Also avoid "risky" foods. Pasta with red sauce is "risky," especially if you are dressed in a white blouse or shirt. Fried chicken may be "tricky." In a restaurant, use a knife and fork to eat fried chicken. At a picnic, use your hands.

This may mean that you forego some of your favorite foods at business meals . . . and that's okay. I absolutely love sushi, but when dining with a client, I never order it. Despite years of practice, I find most pieces of sushi are just too big for me to eat without creating chipmunk cheeks. And inevitably, as soon as I bite down, wasabi hits my nasal passages.

Also, I strongly advise against ordering steamed lobster. First, it's an incredibly messy entrée to eat. Second, at a good number of restaurants, the waitstaff will present diners with bibs to wear while dismembering their crustaceans. Two-year-olds look adorable in bibs. Young professionals do not.

46. Handle mistakes gracefully

If you happen to make a mistake at the dining table, don't worry. Just handle it as gracefully as you can.

If a cherry tomato jumps off your salad plate, discretely pick up the tomato and place it back on your plate.

If you knock over a glass of iced tea, use your napkin to stop the tea from flowing around the table, and immediately ask the waitstaff for help. (By the way, if you knock something over and it stains someone's outfit, you're responsible for their dry cleaning bill.)

If you drop a piece of silverware or some item of food on the floor, and someone might trip or slip on it, quickly inform the waitstaff.

47. Know who pays for business meals

In general, the host pays for the meal. However, let's consider some specific situations:

When you and five other summer associates agree to lunch at the trendy little Mexican restaurant around the corner, plan to pay one-sixth of the total bill. This holds true even if you eat only one fish taco, while everyone else feasts on guacamole and chips, fajitas, and dessert. If you can't afford to subsidize others' lunches, opt out of some group meals and bring your lunch to work.

When a supervisor extends an invitation to lunch, he or she should pick up the tab.

If you ask a senior analyst out to lunch in the hope of receiving some career advice, you have assumed the role of host or hostess. That means you're responsible for paying for your guest's meal as well as your own. However, if your guest indicates that she wishes to pick up the tab, it's okay for her to do so. Just make sure you thank her.

48. Attending other social events

Instead of a meal, you may be invited to a cocktail party or reception. The same rules regarding invitations and R.S.V.P.'s apply: decide whether or not you can attend; communicate your decision as quickly as possible; and once you communicate that you will attend, remember that only an emergency excuses your absence.

To the extent possible, obtain a guest list and do some research before the event. You may discover other guests who have graduated from your school. If so, you have something in common with those people, and this can serve as a starting point for conversations. Maybe you hope to land a job with your host. If your research reveals that members of the hiring committee will be present, the event offers you the opportunity to demonstrate your ability to manage future social interactions with clients. Perhaps your job involves working in a company's marketing department, but your real goal is to work in operations. Researching the invitee list may reveal whether anyone from operations will attend.

Develop a handful of questions that you can ask virtually anyone: What practice group do you work in? What do you like most about the company or firm? Have you always lived in San Francisco? Where have you worked before? Outside of work, what do you do in your spare time?

49. Managing cocktail parties and receptions

When invited to a cocktail party or reception, arrive on time. Find the host or hostess and thank him or her for the invitation. Then, get something in your hands—food or beverage, but never both. Always keep one hand free to shake others' hands.

Everyone who attends social events has a responsibility to mingle. Participate in 10- or 15-minute conversations, and then move on.

To bring a conversation to a close, you might say: "It was great chatting with you. I hope we can stay in touch. I think I'll freshen my drink."

If you have a business or a personal calling card, initiating a card exchange will help bring a conversation to a close. Say: "I'm glad we had the chance to meet and would like to stay in touch. Do you have a business card?"

50. Follow up

After a cocktail party or reception, follow up. At a very minimum, note the names and contact information of the people you met as well as any special interests they expressed.

If you met a potential professional contact, invite that person to "link" to you via LinkedIn.

With your new contacts, reach out and stay in touch. Suggest a future meeting over coffee or lunch. Reference your shared interests. If you both love baseball, each season gives you hundreds of opportunities to reconnect. If you're both into the local restaurant scene, whenever your favorite chef posts a new recipe online, forward it.

If an event takes place in a supervisor's home, send your supervisor a handwritten thank-you note (see #23) to his or her home address.

Chapter 6

Communicating Via Technology

Successful summer associates, interns and new hires communicate professionally. Whether communicating directly or electronically, real professionals use business-appropriate language, and they are always polite.

51. Email professionally

Always remember that any email or text message you send using an organization's computer or smartphone is a business communication.

Draft clear and succinct messages. Use business-appropriate spelling, grammar, and punctuation. Do not rely on spell-check. Do not use texting abbreviations or any other abbreviations that a recipient might not understand.

When drafting email, check the tone of the message. Always use a polite tone that clearly articulates the information you wish to convey. Avoid writing snarky messages.

Carefully review emails before sending them. Consider whether your recipient might misinterpret specific words in your message. Trust me, if any one word can be read positively, negatively or neutrally, readers will always give it the negative interpretation.

With work-related emails, never use emoticons. If you're uncertain whether a reader will understand your humor, don't send the email.

Because emails can easily be forwarded or printed and shared with others, do not use them to discuss confidential information.

52. Start with a salutation

Whenever you initiate an email exchange, use a salutation. A simple opening, such as "Good morning, Jack," is appropriate for people you know well. For people you don't know well or have never met, use a more formal opening, such as "Dear Ms. Smith."

These salutations turn out to be critically important, especially in our fast-paced work world. Some studies have shown that recipients of emails that do not include a salutation interpret the message as being the equivalent of an order or demand. At this point in your career, you are not in a position to give an order to anyone.

As an online communication continues, it is not necessary to begin each new message with a salutation.

53. Emailing your supervisor

Because so many supervising lawyers and supervisors are inundated with emails—receiving hundreds of electronic messages on any given day—send only those emails that are critical to the completion of your tasks and assignments.

When assigned to a group project, determine who needs to be involved in email exchanges. Cc: or bcc: supervisors only when it is absolutely necessary that they receive the information contained within.

When a supervisor assigns three summer associates, interns or new hires to complete a document review, each of the employees might send an email to the supervisor indicating that he or she has received and understands the assignment. However, the supervisor need not be copied on emails among the employees as they arrange when and where they will tackle the project.

54. Close professionally

End all business emails with a business-appropriate closing followed by your name. At work, use "sincerely" or "regards." When you email someone you don't know, sign off using your first and last name.

55. Use an email signature line

Work with your organization's technology department to set up your email account. It should include a formal signature line that appears at the bottom of all your outgoing emails. Your signature line should include your name, position in the organization, work phone number, and cell phone number. This makes it easy for recipients to get in touch with you. It might look something like this:

Matthew Lane
Summer Intern
Luxury Goods Management Firm
Ph: (212) 385-2196
Cell: (656) 221-9785

56. Confirm your employer's expectations regarding email response time

In most organizations, employees are expected to reply to emails by the end of the day in which the email was received. However, in some organizations, workers may be expected to reply to emails within two hours of receipt. Understand and conform to your supervisor's expectations regarding email response time.

When sending emails to a supervisor, don't hold her to this same two-hour standard. Since your supervisor may receive hundreds of emails each day, she may not be able to respond to each one on a daily basis.

If you require a response from a supervisor, be prepared to follow up with a second email. Craft this message carefully.

Avoid writing: "Hey, I told you I couldn't finish this analysis until you give me last month's data."

Instead, write: Some quick follow-up. In order for me to complete the annual analysis, I need to receive last month's data from you. Please let me know when you anticipate finalizing it. Immediately upon its receipt, I'll complete and file my report.

57. Respond to all email requests

At the end of each day, reply to every email and voicemail message you have received.

Caveat: when someone leaves you a voicemail message indicating that a reply is not needed, you do not need to respond. However, when someone sends an email with an indication that it is "FYI," confirm your receipt of the message by replying with a simple "thank you."

At the end of the day, if you do not have an answer to an email or voicemail request, provide a status update. Before leaving work, you might email your supervisor an update like this:

I received your email earlier today and immediately began to assemble all of the newly discovered evidence that should prove Smith's innocence. I am waiting for one DNA report, which I should receive first thing tomorrow. I will stay on top of this and inform you as soon as I have everything in hand.

58. Never use a company computer or smartphone to share gossip, jokes, or snarky remarks

Do not use email to say anything about a fellow employee, client or customer that you would not say to that person face to face.

If you're in doubt as to whether you should say something in an email or text message—if anything in the back of your mind or gut makes you hesitate, do not hit SEND. Please step away from your laptop, tablet or smartphone.

Every year, every month—dare I write, every day—someone's career ends because he or she carelessly sent an email or text message.

Remember, anything and everything you write in an email or text message can be printed and given to your employer. It can also become a permanent part of your employment record.

59. Always communicate professionally on the phone

Answer every phone call with a greeting: "Good morning, this is Susan Smith in Finance. May I help you?"

Before you place a phone call, especially a call made on your supervisor's behalf, know exactly what you wish to say. If necessary, write out a script and use it.

Should you need to leave a voicemail message, state your name, the nature of your call, and a return phone number in a polite and succinct manner. Because few people can record information as quickly as you can speak, repeat your name and phone number.

Even if you happen to communicate primarily through email or text messaging, please do not create a voicemail greeting that says: "I don't respond to voicemail messages. Please text me instead." This message is rude. It suggests the person who made the recording feels he or she is more important than everyone else.

Remember, you are starting your professional life. Always demonstrate your ability to flex to the wants, needs and communication preferences of others.

60. Get comfortable with technology

The more comfortable and proficient you become with technology at work, the more valuable you become to the organization. Learn how to transfer phone calls and how to establish conference calls. Understand the logistics required to set up a videoconference.

Similarly, become familiar with all software regularly used by members of your organization, including Word, Excel, PowerPoint, and more. Learn how to scan documents and email large files. Become comfortable with tracking changes within a document. If your employer uses a cloud data storage system, understand how to access the cloud.

If you are asked to perform a task that requires the use of technology, and if you are unfamiliar with the particular equipment or software, admit your unfamiliarity up front. Then, get familiar fast:

I understand you need me to phone the reporter with The New York Times *and then connect you to that call. I've never done that before. It'll take me one minute to work with the office manager and learn how to do this. I'll have you connected as quickly as possible.*

Chapter 7

Building Your Network

It's never too early to start building a professional network. Look for people who can help you accomplish day-to-day tasks, as well as people who can help you think and plan your future. Commit to building and nurturing these relationships.

61. Start building your network today

Too many young professionals discount the importance of building their networks. This is a huge mistake. I've worked with junior partners in law and consulting firms who have been thrust into positions in which they are expected to develop new business. When we meet, all too frequently the partners tell me, "I guess I need to start building my network." I always want to reply, "It's almost too late. You should have started building your network while you were still in school."

It's never too early to start building your networks, and everyone you meet is a possible candidate for inclusion.

62. Build multiple networks

As soon as you enter the workplace, you should start building three separate networks:

Operational – Identify a group of people at work who can help you accomplish specific work-related tasks. When a senior lawyer asks you to compose a memorandum regarding the legal issues an entrepreneur should consider in the early stages of incorporation, who should you phone in the firm's law library? Who can you phone in IT when an Excel spreadsheet suddenly disappears from your computer's desktop? Have you been tasked with developing company profiles? Who can show you how to quickly access financial statements?

Strategic – Identify a group of people who can help you think through your career goals and strategies for accomplishing them. Who can explain both typical and atypical career paths and milestones against which you can measure your success?

Personal – Identify a group of people who can help you address issues that arise in your personal life. After a breakup with your girlfriend or boyfriend, who is the first person you'll text? When you want to head to the gym for a particularly hard workout, who always helps you get through that last set of reps? When you just want someone to listen to you dream, who can you call?

63. Networking = relationship-building

Lots of people cringe at the thought of building a network. They think of "networking" as "schmoozing," and they believe it involves attending events and pushing themselves upon others.

If this is what you believe, let's set your thinking straight! From now on, when you think "networking," think "relationship-building." Networking entails meeting another individual, either in person or online, having some sort of exchange, and determining whether there's a basis for a second exchange. That's it!

Look for everyday opportunities to connect with people as people, and slowly but surely, you will build a network.

Want a networking success story? Here's one:

As soon as Kevin Systrom and Mike Krieger released their photo-sharing app Instagram, thousands began to download it. The app became so popular that the computer systems handling the photos frequently crashed. Systrom immediately knew he needed help. He scrolled through the contacts on his phone until he found the name of Adam D'Angelo, a former chief technology officer at Facebook. They had met seven years earlier . . . at a Stanford University fraternity party.

What advice does Systrom give to would-be entrepreneurs today? He tells them to make every effort to meet and get to know other people.

64. Be prepared to tell your story

For those of us who are introverted, talking about ourselves can be a real challenge. Overcome that challenge by planning what you will and will not say. Create two or three sentences that describe who you are and what you do.

As you create these sentences, aim for simplicity over complexity. What do you wish to emphasize about who you are?

Want to demonstrate that you're persistent? Tell me about how you took on a particularly tough research project—and would not give up until you spoke with the CEO of the company.

Want to show that you're a team player? Tell me about the spring break where you worked with a group to help rebuild a community devastated by storms.

Be prepared to enthusiastically speak about yourself. If you've had a bad day at work, clear every negative thought from your mind before you head out to connect with others.

65. Show a genuine interest in others

Develop some questions that you can ask virtually anyone. How do you get into work everyday? Subway? Drive? How long is your commute? Did you get stuck in last week's storm? Where will you go on vacation this year? As people respond, listen and ask appropriate follow-up questions.

A special note for introverts: these questions may be the most useful tool in your networking toolkit. Most people love to talk about themselves. To the extent you ask questions that encourage others to speak, you will be considered a brilliant conversationalist.

At all of these events, keep in mind that your primary goal in any conversation is to find a reason to have a second conversation. Today's conversation may lead to coffee in a few weeks, a lunch by the end of the summer, and a job offer next year.

66. Stay in touch

Networks can be fragile. Remember, they involve relationships with other people, and some people require more attention than others. Once you've invested time in building a relationship, don't let that relationship wither and die.

How do you keep in touch? If you've returned to school, before fall finals begin, consider sending quick emails to special contacts that say something like: "Before finals begin, I just wanted to reach out and wish you a happy holiday."

Take advantage of slower times at work to reconnect with key contacts. Offer to take a contact out for a cup of coffee or quick lunch so that you can learn the latest happenings at work. It's possible a position has just opened up for which you are particularly qualified.

67. Build diverse networks

Don't limit your network to people who are just like you. Connect with people who are much older—friends of your parents, for example, or your teachers and professors. Connect with people who have interests different from your own. They may expose you to opportunities that you otherwise might not have considered.

Keep in mind the example of Bill Gates and Warren Buffet—two men who couldn't be more different. Their relationship started when the still-relatively-young Microsoft CEO approached the oracle of Omaha. Buffet initially told Gates he knew nothing about software and wasn't particularly interested in learning about it. Gates replied that Buffet's lack of interest didn't bother him one bit. The two ended up bonding over games of bridge.

These two very different people have now joined forces and are changing the world of philanthropy. They will likely succeed, mostly because Gates made the effort to connect with someone with whom he first appeared to share little in common.

68. Carry business cards

If your employer does not provide you with a business card, create a personal card that includes the following information: your name, your personal email address, and your phone number. If you are student, you may also list the name of your school and your anticipated graduation date.

Any office supply store or print shop can produce hundreds of these cards at a minimal cost. Alternatively, if you have access to a computer and printer, you can create them on your own.

Because you never know when you might encounter someone who you would like to add to your network, carry your business or personal cards with you at all times.

And yes, carry these cards even if you have an online presence on Facebook and LinkedIn. Believe it or not, some people, including people you want and need to know, are not active in the world of social networking. As long as you carry a business card with you at all times, you always have the ability to exchange contact information.

69. Face-to-face networking

Take a lead from the world of high tech and place yourself in positions where you must interact with other people face to face. Apple founder Steve Jobs understood the critical importance of serendipitous encounters. When building the Apple campus, he actively worked with architects to design opportunities for people to bump into each other. He knew that random conversations often play a critical role in innovation.

Similarly, Yahoo! CEO Marissa Mayer recently placed limits on telecommuting, telling her company's employees, "Some of the best decisions and insights come from hallway and cafeteria discussions, meeting new people, and impromptu team meetings."

If you are active in the world of social networking, by all means, continue. However, never underestimate the potential importance and value of an unplanned face-to-face connection.

70. Social networking

Social networking gives you the opportunity to connect directly with hiring managers, recruiters and entrepreneurs. It also allows you to develop a community of colleagues and mentors. So by all means, establish an online presence on various social networking sites.

Post comments on Twitter and LinkedIn, create a blog or post a video that demonstrates your unique knowledge of a particular subject area. As you acquire new skills and abilities, post updates. Use social networking to keep others apprised of your short- and long-term goals.

Thinking about creating your personal brand? Social networking allows you to share your passions. LinkedIn, Twitter and other social networking sites may be the perfect venues for you to market yourself to people who are in search of your expertise.

However, as an intern, summer associate or new hire, before you post anything online, make sure you understand your employer's social networking policies. Unless you receive specific authorization, do not post anything about your employer, fellow employees, customers or clients. If you've been hired to blog or tweet about an industry, show discretion and write professionally. The Internet is replete with examples of people who have lost their jobs in 140 characters or less.

Chapter 8

Dressing For Work

Employers expect interns, summer associates and new hires to dress in a work-appropriate manner. If you happen to take a position in a fashion-forward industry, plan to dress in a manner that demonstrates your understanding of fashion. (Watch *The Devil Wears Prada*.) If you happen to land an internship or job in a high-tech startup, you may be able to wear jeans and a hoodie to work. (Watch *The Social Network*.) Fit in by dressing the way your coworkers dress.

71. Make a good first impression

You have only one opportunity to make a first impression, and you will make it incredibly fast. In fact, studies indicate that people develop first impressions within a matter of seconds.

Part of any first impression you make will be based upon what you say. As a result, it's critical that you always speak in a professional manner.

The remainder of any first impression you make will be based upon your physical appearance, including your attire.

Whenever you dress for work or a social event sponsored by your employer, choose an outfit that is business-appropriate.

Above all, make sure the outfits you wear to work are neat and clean. They should never be overly revealing or sexually provocative. Do not wear party clothes to work. Cover up sundresses with a sweater. In most cases, save jeans and T-shirts for your weekends. Avoid sneakers, very high heels, and flip-flops.

72. Dress for your employer's culture

Every organization has a culture, and employees of the organization express that culture through their dress. As a summer associate, intern or new hire, one of your goals is to fit into the organizational culture by dressing in a like manner.

If you've landed a job with a PR firm that represents several high-fashion designers, you need to quickly build a fashion-forward wardrobe. Alternatively, if you've landed a summer internship on Capitol Hill, be prepared to dress in conservative suits. If you're about to start work with an Internet startup, you may get away with wearing jeans and T-shirts every day.

In virtually every work culture, please avoid wearing the following mistakes:

- torn, dirty or frayed clothing;
- clothing bearing words or images that others might find offensive;
- clothing that reveals cleavage or excessive chest hair;
- clothing that reveals whale tails or plumber's cracks!

73. Dress for the job you want

If your long-term goal is to become the director of marketing with a nonprofit, wear outfits similar to those worn by the most senior people on the marketing team. If your goal is to eventually land a position in a large consulting firm, dress as the most successful consultants do. If your ultimate goal is to become a spokesperson for a member of Congress, observe the current spokesperson's attire and dress similarly.

This process of always thinking onward and upward may be the most exciting thing about starting your career. Enjoy it! Dream about who and what you want to become. Study the people who have achieved the level of excellence to which you aspire. And then go for it . . . like crazy! Every time you get comfortable with where you are, know that it's time to challenge yourself to move on.

74. Hair

One of the first features people notice is your hair—not whether you have it or not, but how neatly you keep your hair styled. Before you head into work, wash, dry, and style your hair. Once or twice during the day, confirm that every hair is still in place.

Find a style that ensures hair does not fall into your face during the course of meetings.

Avoid unconsciously playing with your hair throughout the workday.

75. Shoes

Most employers also notice the status of your shoes. Are they shined? Have the heels been worn down? Are they nicked or otherwise marred?

Before you head to work, look down. If your shoes don't look like those worn by the leaders in your industry, change into something else.

Caveat: if you walk to work or have a long commute, you may wear more comfortable shoes during your travels to and from work. However, before you arrive at work, switch into business-appropriate shoes.

76. Take good grooming seriously

Your hands and your nails should be clean. Bathe daily. Wear deodorant or antiperspirant.

If you wear makeup, keep it light. Avoid heavy eye shadow or dark lipstick, unless, of course, that's the standard in the organization where you work.

Avoid over-spritzing cologne or perfume. Many people are allergic to or bothered by strong scents.

Create an emergency kit that contains any personal hygiene items you might need during the course of a work day: comb, dental floss, toothbrush and paste, stain removal stick, a few safety pins, and for women, a tampon.

Always wash your hands before lunch and after you eat. Use the mirror in the restroom to confirm that none of your lunch is stuck in your teeth.

77. After-work attire

In most cases, when you are invited to a post-workday social event, the clothing you have worn to work is also appropriate for the event.

For other business-related social events, when determining what to wear, check the invitation.

Where "business attire" is specified, a nice office outfit should be perfect.

If "festive attire" is specified—as the invitation may read for an office holiday party—feel free to add a little sparkle or a holiday pin or tie.

Should you be invited to a "black tie" event, gentlemen should wear a tux and ladies should think . . . elegance. Ladies may wear a floor-length dress, a cocktail dress or even slacks as long as the outfit communicates *I've dressed up for this event.*

78. Stash a back-up outfit at work

In addition to your emergency kit, plan for unexpected events by storing a back-up outfit at work.

During the course of a business lunch, a member of the waitstaff may inadvertently spill some food on you. As long as you have a backup outfit at work, you can quickly change clothes and feel comfortable that you look professional throughout the afternoon.

If business casual attire is the standard for your workplace, consider making a typical "interview outfit" your backup outfit. (Depending on your industry, this may be a suit.) Should you be invited to attend a client meeting, a business development pitch, a fashion preview, a Senate hearing, etc., you can quickly switch outfits and dress your best.

79. Cover up tattoos and body studs

B e aware that some employers (and lots of clients and customers) may be uncomfortable with excessive tattoos and body studs. In some cases, you may need to cover them up.

If you've landed an internship or new job with *Chopper* magazine, no one will look twice at tattoos or body studs. However, if you're just about to start work at a very conservative accounting firm, cover up your tattoos and remove all body studs except earrings.

Verbal communication is critical to every employee's success. Remove any tongue studs that keep you from speaking clearly.

If you do not have a tattoo, fight off the urge to get one. "Tattoo regret" is all too common, and removing a tattoo is costly, uncomfortable, and time-consuming.

80. Beware of casual dress

As a summer associate, intern or new hire, one of your goals is to become memorable to key decision-makers within the organization. Do everything necessary to avoid being remembered as the person who dresses more casually or sloppily than anyone else.

You may be amazed to learn how little is required to earn this distinction. Three years after the fact, I still hear about a summer associate in Atlanta who decided he did not need to wear socks into the office. The impression he created was not a positive one.

So, make the effort. Dress to impress. By your appearance, let everyone you encounter know that you are serious about attending to lots of little details, including the details of your appearance.

Chapter 9

Separating Your Work & Your Personal Life

You will discover that work can occupy your life 24/7. Demonstrate a commitment to your employer and to the organization's goals. However, don't become a workaholic. You have lots of years ahead of you to invest in your career.

Understand your employer's expectations regarding availability and accessibility. Then, set aside time for family and friends.

81. Show up

Once you join the workforce, you are expected to attend work every day.

If you become ill, inform your supervisor as quickly as possible. Provide updates indicating when you anticipate returning to work. Then, stay home. No one appreciates a work colleague who spreads germs and disease.

When you are at work, be fully present. Avoid checking your personal email accounts. Stash you iPod.

In an effort to alleviate workplace stress, some employers encourage their workers to briefly visit Facebook and other social networking sites throughout the day. Don't abuse this privilege. A supervisor or supervising lawyer should never discover that you're updating your Facebook status when you should be tackling tasks.

Work at your assigned workstation or desk. If you need to leave your work area, tell your supervisor or a coworker where you will be and when you intend to return.

82. Manage personal emergencies

Once you enter the workforce, you may encounter a personal emergency. On a morning walk, your dog may break free from its leash. Or a parent may unexpectedly become ill, and you're the only one at home who can rush him or her to the hospital. When an emergency arises, immediately inform your supervisor, quickly address the emergency, and then, as soon as possible, return to work.

Some emergencies may require an extended commitment of your time. In these cases, work closely with your supervisor to manage his or her expectations. Depending on the nature of the emergency, you may also wish to reach out to HR, whose staff can help you navigate the organization's policies and procedures as well as special benefits that may be mandated by law, such as the Family and Medical Leave Act.

Avoid making personal phone calls at work. If you need to make an emergency phone call, do so during your lunch break.

83. Separate professional and personal social networking

Use separate social networking sites for business and social contacts. Consider using LinkedIn for work-related and business contacts and Facebook as the social networking site you use to stay in touch with families and friends.

If a supervisor or someone else at work asks you to "friend" them on Facebook, think long and hard before doing so. If you agree to this request, you give your supervisor or coworker permission to access every piece of data you post there. Consider telling people at work that you reserve Facebook solely as a means to stay in touch with family and friends. Then, invite them to link to you via LinkedIn.

Even if you separate your networks, assume anything you post on Facebook eventually will be viewed by someone at work. Do you want your supervisor to surmise that the reason you called in sick this morning had something to do with last night's party? Do you want HR and everyone else in the world to see spring break photos of you in a bikini or Speedo?

Remember, anything you post online may be discovered by a current or future employer.

Be discrete. Be careful. Be professional.

84. Do not blog, tweet or post anything about your employer

Additionally, do not blog, tweet or post on a social networking site anything about the people with whom you work. It's bad manners, and it may place you in violation of your organization's confidentiality policy.

Do not post anything online that someone might find offensive. After discovering offensive or inappropriate postings, corporations, law firms and other organizations have withdrawn job offers and dismissed employees.

Remember, anything you post online lives forever.

85. Attend office parties

You may be invited to participate in office birthday parties or some other office celebrations. Enjoy yourself. Sign the birthday card, and eat a piece of cake.

If birthday celebrations are not the norm at your employer, keep your birthday plans private. If you have developed friendships at work, save any birthday celebrations for after-work hours. Any gift exchange should take place away from work.

As for other business-related social gatherings, every organization I know has at least one nightmare story about an employee who said or did something inappropriate after consuming too much alcohol. Some of these employees have been able to survive such unfortunate incidents because they are workers who have a history of superlative performance and significant contributions to the organization's bottom line. Their one bad act is viewed as an anomaly. Others, however, struggle with a nasty story that continues to haunt them in their professional lives.

Every office party is, first and foremost, a business event. Act in a business-appropriate manner.

86. Office gifts

When an office collection is taken up to purchase a gift for an employee, are summer associates, interns and new hires expected to contribute? Absolutely not for summer associates and interns, probably not for new hires.

If you would like to contribute, make a small donation. However, junior employees are never expected to purchase gifts for their supervisors or for more senior employees.

The same rule applies to holiday gifts.

If a supervisor presents you with a gift, express genuine appreciation and follow up with a handwritten thank-you note (see #23). Ideally, write and send the thank-you note within 48 hours of receiving the gift.

87. Do not date coworkers

Dating fellow employees creates all sorts of problems and concerns. Supervisors may wonder whether you and your coworker are fully focused on your work and assigned tasks. They may be concerned that a personal disagreement will spill over into the work place. Interoffice relationships may also give rise to specific legal issues. So, don't do it!

Once you've decided to disregard my advice, check with HR to confirm your employer's policies regarding relationships with fellow employees.

Finally, sit down with your new significant other and have a serious discussion about how you will behave in the office. At a minimum, you should agree to the following:

- No public displays of affection in the office.

- Keep all office communications professional, and limit the number of in-office emails and phone calls the two of you exchange.

- Pre-determine how you will manage your day-to-day working relationship should the personal relationship disintegrate.

88. Be prepared to set boundaries

Technology allows us to stay connected 24/7/365. While remaining connected with people at work is sometimes critical, it can also impinge upon personal relationships.

With your supervisor, clarify expectations regarding your availability.

When discussing your availability, make sure you understand whether your employer expects you to be physically present, or whether electronic availability will suffice. One of my law firm contacts shared the following nightmare scenario:

During a Friday afternoon conference call, a litigation team determined they needed to work throughout the weekend to finalize a series of documents. The partner in charge of the case arrived at the office early Saturday morning. She waited for a particular new associate to arrive. When the newest member of the team failed to show, the partner checked her emails and discovered a message from the junior lawyer that read something like this: "I will be in New Orleans throughout the weekend. Just scan and email the documents to me, and I will work on them remotely."

To say that the partner went ballistic would not be an exaggeration. Beyond not meeting the partner's expectations—that everyone would work in the Houston office throughout the weekend—the junior lawyer's request to have documents scanned and forwarded increased the partner's workload. The entire fiasco could have been avoided had the new associate spoken with the partner before heading out of town.

89. Be fully present

Just as you should be fully present at work, when you are with family and friends, give them your undivided attention. Unless you expect an emergency phone call, email or text, turn off your smartphone. Enjoy a conversation with Mom or Dad or your best friend without the distraction of emails and texts. Set aside an hour to read without interruption. Grab some exercise or a bite to eat and leave your smartphone behind. Don't worry. You'll live.

Periodically unplugging from the workplace may be one of the most important things you do for your own mental health. In order to fully recharge, your brain requires a certain amount of undisturbed free time. So, turn off your electronic gear, especially when you head to bed.

And if you happen to believe that you're a superlative multitasker—someone who can text friends while simultaneously completing complex financials analyses—think again. Studies consistently find that very few people are able to tackle several tasks at one time and manage all of them well. Other studies indicate that multitaskers are not as productive as their singularly focused counterparts.

90. Know when to put your professional persona on hold

Some of the skills that will help make you a successful professional are not necessarily the same skills that will make you a cherished friend or life partner.

The Capitol Hill intern who wishes to become a successful politician should avoid giving lengthy speeches to friends and family. Similarly, the new hire working in the world of high fashion should avoid offering unrequested advice about the attire of friends and family members.

Throughout your personal and professional life, incorporate a little humility. Show some modesty. Avoid pretense. Recognize that anything you accomplish will be the result of your own efforts combined with the contributions of parents, educators, mentors, fellow employees, clients and customers. Show some quiet confidence, and let others discover the depths of your ability.

Chapter 10

When Your Internship Ends

Once your time as a summer associate or intern ends, you still have work to do. Think about how you can use the time you've invested as a springboard to future professional opportunities. Begin building a professional portfolio. Continue creating your professional network. Start thinking about what's next and all the possibilities that lie ahead.

91. Your last day of work

On the last day of your summer associate program or internship, complete every project or task that was assigned to you. If possible, meet with your supervisor and review the status of projects and tasks.

If you have been assigned some portion of a larger project and others will continue to work on that project after you leave, transfer your work product to another team member. Outline the task that you were assigned. Describe how you tackled the task and the results you obtained. If a task required you to connect with people beyond team members, create a list of those contacts, their email addresses and phone numbers, and their specific contributions.

In Chapter 2, we discussed the importance of creating a great first impression. The last impressions you create are of equal importance. If you leave assigned work undone or fail to satisfactorily transfer your work to a responsible colleague, the entire work team could be negatively affected. Make sure that final impressions about your work remain positive.

92. Complete your summer associate or internship journal

Throughout your time as a summer associate or intern, and if you've followed my advice, you've kept a paper or electronic journal (see #2 and #31). Now that your introduction to the world of work is about to end, don't make the mistake of tossing your journal into a drawer or filing it away on your desktop. Instead, use this information to start building your professional brand. Identify how you are now unique and distinguishable from every other person in the world because of the projects you've tackled, the lessons you've learned, and the new goals and objectives you've set.

As you advance in your career, you will need to be able to describe:

- who you are;
- why you seek a particular result (a job offer, IPO funding, leadership assignment); and
- how you plan to achieve that result.

Of these three issues, the "why" is the most important. Why do you wish to enter the world of high stakes litigation? Why does the world of corporate finance intrigue you? Why are you fascinated by a new philanthropic model and do you truly believe it will result in more people receiving aid? Your journal will help you explore and answer your "why" questions.

93. If possible, retain work samples

Ask your supervisor whether you may retain a copy of any work you've produced. (Never assume that you may keep your work. Anything you produce at work is the property of your employer.) Did you help create a document detailing the latest developments in cybersecurity? Ask if you may retain a copy of your final report. Did you help build a financial justification for a new product launch? Ask whether you may keep a copy for future reference.

Use these materials to begin building your professional portfolio.

94. Ask your supervisor to serve as a future reference

Request a letter of reference from your supervisor that you can share with future prospective employers.

95. Express your thanks

Thank every member of the staff who helped you throughout your summer associate program or internship. Stop by HR and express appreciation for the opportunities you have been provided.

With regard to supervisors, handwrite a thank-you note (see #23). You may leave it with this person on your last day or mail it to the office within two days of your last day of work.

When you draft this note, make it personal. Don't just say, "Thanks very much for your help this summer." Instead, be very specific. Identify one or two things your supervisor did or said, and note how and why they were important to your growth and development.

96. Review the goals you set at the beginning of your program

If you accomplished all of your goals, it's time to set some new ones.

And it's definitely time to think about your next internship or your first job. Think about what you learned as the result of your internship or time as a summer associate. Did you acquire new knowledge? New skills? Given your professional goals, what additional skills or knowledge do you still need to acquire?

I cannot overemphasize how important I believe goal-setting to be. All the people I know who have achieved real success in their careers have engaged in rigorous goal-setting. Throughout their lives, they have constantly reevaluated and re-prioritized their goals.

Set both professional and personal stretch goals—the kind of goals that seem nearly impossible to achieve. These will push you beyond your comfort zone and teach you new lessons.

My personal stretch goal one year included running a marathon. It was a huge stretch, given that I could barely run a mile when I set the goal. Over many months of training, I learned that I could achieve even the most extreme goal by breaking the challenge into manageable tasks. Today, I own a medal that proves I completed a 26.2-mile run.

97. Stay in touch

Commit to staying in touch with fellow interns and summer associates, your supervisor, and key staff members. If you have linked to them via LinkedIn, staying in touch should be pretty easy. It just requires conscious effort on your part.

If you served as an intern/executive assistant to a fashion magazine editor—and you know the editor will travel to Paris next month for the spring couture shows—set aside some time to surf the web, find the newest, latest, greatest restaurant in Paris, and forward that information to the editor. If you worked as a Capitol Hill intern and learn your member of Congress has played a critical role in some recently passed legislation, send him or her a congratulatory email.

Every few months, reach out to the members of your network. Share your most recent accomplishments, and more importantly, show a genuine interest in their successes and challenges.

98. Never burn a bridge

Hopefully, you will enjoy every minute of your time as a summer associate, intern or new hire; and every person you encounter. However, you may encounter someone who, at best, is not helpful and, at worst, is destructive.

No matter how unpleasant someone may be, do not respond in kind. Shrug off their behavior and move on.

Caveat: if the actions of a supervisor or coworker constitute a "hostile work environment," i.e., you feel harassed or are afraid to go to work because of an offensive, intimidating or oppressive environment created by a harasser, immediately contact HR.

99. Pass it on

Now that you know what it takes to succeed, help others who follow. Offer to serve as a mentor to the person who will fill your internship position next year. Share everything you learned about the culture of a law firm with next year's summer associates. And once you become wildly successful, create internships for others and mentor every summer associate you encounter.

100. Celebrate!

You have begun what I hope will be a lifelong commitment to learning as a professional. Be prepared for some incredible challenges. Keep going strong. Every time you cross a hurdle, give yourself a high five. The people who get ahead work smart and hard. Good luck!

About the Author

A graduate of the University of Missouri and George Washington University Law School, Mary Crane lobbied in Washington D.C. for nearly ten years before pursuing her lifelong interests in food and wine. She enrolled in the Culinary Institute of America, and upon graduation, worked at the White House as an assistant chef. During this time, Crane discovered the important relationships between food, wine, and business. Her desire to share this unique knowledge yielded Mary Crane & Associates.

Today, Mary Crane travels North America delivering high-impact, high-energy programs to Fortune 500 companies, leading law firms, nonprofits and colleges and universities. She helps students, interns and new hires successfully make the critically important transition from school to work.

Mary Crane has been featured on *60 Minutes*, *Fox Business News*, and ABC Radio. She has been quoted extensively in a variety of print and electronic media, including *The New York Times*, *The Wall Street Journal*, Forbes.com, Fortune.com, and CNN.com.

Made in the USA
San Bernardino, CA
19 May 2014